THE ROCKEFELLER CENTER
CHRISTMAS TREE

THE ROCKEFELLER CENTER CHRISTMAS TREE

THE ROCKEFELLER CENTER CHRISTMAS TREE

The History & Lore of the World's Most Famous Evergreen

By Nancy Armstrong

Edited by Alexandra Lewis

CIDER MILL PRESS

BOOK PUBLISHERS

Kennebunkport, Maine

13-Digit ISBN: 978-1-60433-101-1
10-Digit ISBN: 1-60433-101-1

This book may be ordered by mail from the publisher. Please include $2.95 for postage and handling.

Please support your local bookseller first!

Books published by Cider Mill Press Book Publishers are available at special discounts for bulk purchases in the United States by corporations, institutions, and other organizations. For more information, please contact the publisher.

Cider Mill Press Book Publishers
"Where good books are ready for press"
12 Port Farm Road
Kennebunkport, Maine 04046
Visit us on the web!
www.cidermillpress.com

Designed by PonderosaPineDesign.com, Vicky Vaughn Shea

Typography: Adobe Caslon, Dingbats, Linotype Decorations, Love Letter Typewriter, Olduvai, Salmiak, Seria Sans

Photo & iIllustration credits: cover, page 6 Xinhua/Landov; cover, page 9 ©www.Shutterstock.com/Mario Bruno; back cover, page 138 ©iStockphoto.com/Shawn Gearhart; back cover ©iStockphoto.com/Tomasz Pietryszek; back cover Jorge Moro; back cover flap ©iStockphoto.com/Boris Yankov. All interior photos up to 1995 ©Rockefeller Group, Inc. ©2008, after 1996 ©Tishman Speyer Rockefeller Center ©2008. With the exception of: page 8 ©www.Shutterstock.com/Nialat; page 9, 13 ©www.Shutterstock.com/Karlionau; page 10 ©www.Shutterstock.com/mvprint; page 19 ©iStockphoto.com/Rafal Fabrykiewicz; page 23 ©www.Shutterstock.com/Travis Manley; page 28 ©www.Shutterstock.com/Alan Linn; page 31 ©www.Shutterstock.com/Eric Isselée; page 41 ©www.Shutterstock.com/Yury Asotov; page 53 ©www.Shutterstock.com/Petrov Stanislav Eduardovich; page 60 ©www.Shutterstock.com/Patricia A. Phillips; page 63 ©www.Shutterstock.com/FloridaStock; page 73 ©www.Shutterstock.com/Kavram; page 74 ©www.Shutterstock.com/Gregory James Van Raalte; page 107 Marc Averette; page 120, 125 ©www.Shutterstock.com/Andrew F. Kazmierski; page 123 Leando Karunungan http://flickr.com/scubapup; page 128 ©www.Shutterstock.com/David N. Madden; page 130 ©iStockphoto.com/appleuzr

Printed in China

1 2 3 4 5 6 7 8 9 0

First Edition

TABLE OF CONTENTS

Acknowledgments   11

CHAPTER 1   The Beginning   13

CHAPTER 2   A Tradition is Born   17
The 1930s   20

CHAPTER 3   A Tradition Matures   27
The 1940s   30

CHAPTER 4   Tradition and Prosperity   39
The 1950s   42

CHAPTER 5   Keeping up with Tradition   51
The 1960s   54

CHAPTER 6   Tradition Goes Green   61
The 1970s   64

CHAPTER 7   Men of Tradition   71
             The 1980s   77

CHAPTER 8   Tradition in the
             Modern Era   83
             The 1990s   86

CHAPTER 9   Tradition Today   105
             The 2000s   109

CHAPTER 10   The Future   127

Appendix: A Tree Timeline   131
List of Works Consulted   139

ACKNOWLEDGMENTS

This book could not have been completed without the generous help and support of several people. First and foremost, I wish to thank Christine Roussel, archivist at Rockefeller Center, a fascinating and intelligent person who has an odd and sometimes lonely job. Her impressive organization and entertaining insights were instrumental in bringing this book to fruition. Also deserving thanks are Alexandra Lewis and Vicky Vaughn Shea; without their keen eyes and creativity, this book would never have made it to press. My deepest gratitude goes to the friends and family members who have listened to me talk about Christmas trees all spring, but most of all, to Jack Curran, who tolerates me through the solitary and often frustrating process of writing a book better than most and provides endless moral support.

Workers lined up in front of the first Rockefeller Center Christmas tree to collect their hard-earned wages on December 24, 1931.

Chapter 1

The Beginning

On December 24, 1931, Rockefeller Center was not much more than a gaping hole between 49th and 50th streets in Midtown Manhattan. The average onlooker would likely have passed by with little more than a dull glance, unaware that the foundation work had begun on one of the most ambitious private building at that time. Even if he had known, however, he may have been indifferent, for he had a more pressing concern weighing on his mind: a worldwide economic downturn. By the time the center's construction began, the country was waist-deep in the Great Depression, and New York City seemed to feel the crippling effects of this economic crisis more

In December of 1933, the Paulist Choristers opened a week of Christmas caroling and other musical performances at the foot of the majestic Rockefeller Center Christmas tree.

than any other city in the country. Unemployment figures were staggering, and sixty-four percent of New York's construction workers were jobless. For the most part, construction had come to a halt across the city. But John D. Rockefeller Jr.'s center, which would comprise nine main buildings and two smaller structures, created jobs for thousands of people, people who were so thankful to have work that they took it upon themselves to erect the very first Christmas tree in Rockefeller Center.

> *As each man approached the clerk, who was standing next to the tree distributing the wages, he must have thought himself a part of a true Christmas miracle.*

That first tree was a simple twenty-foot balsam, which the workers draped with makeshift garlands and tin cans as decoration. Its presence imbued a festive air to an already celebratory experience as the men lined up next to the tree to receive their paychecks that Christmas Eve in 1931. For some, it was their first paycheck in weeks, if not months. As each man approached the clerk, who was standing next to the tree distributing the wages, he must have thought himself a part of a true Christmas miracle.

Looking back, over seventy-five years later, this

auspicious beginning of a much beloved and storied tradition seems almost too heart-warming to be true, and yet this is actually the way it all began. In the years that followed, technological advances, environmental awareness, national television exposure, and even contributions from gardening experts have made the Rockefeller Center Christmas tree an

extreme spectacle, a much bigger production than that first celebration in 1931. Throughout the tradition's nearly eight decades, though, the spirit of that first tree has endured. It was—and continues to be—a symbol of joy, peace, and, most of all, hope for the millions of people who gaze at it every year during the holiday season.

In 1935, an eighty-foot tree sparked brilliantly in front of the RCA building.

Chapter 2

A Tradition is Born

he Norway spruce has been the variety of evergreen most often selected as the Rockefeller Center Christmas tree since the tradition began. The reason? This species of spruce grows to daunting heights, often more than one hundred feet tall, and it continues to mature throughout its impressive lifespan of eighty to one hundred years. The spruce also grows fairly quickly, at a rate of about one foot per year.

The Norway spruce is not native to North America but to Northern Europe. In the states it is generally planted ornamentally, perhaps as a reminder of our European ancestry. Because it does not grow among other trees in the forest, the Norway spruce flourishes as a full, dense tree that has no trouble meeting the center's minimum width requirement of thirty-five feet at its broadest point. The height minimum is sixty-five feet, but center officials generally aim for seventy-five to ninety feet, with thick, full sets of branches.

As you can imagine, this beloved tree—the most celebrated tree of the holiday season—is selected with great care every year. There are several different ways that a tree can become *the* tree: Rockefeller Center officials may spot a tree on a scouting expedition and approach its owners about donating it, or tree owners may alert center officials that they possess a tree that deserves the honor of becoming the famed Rockefeller Center Christmas tree.

Rockefeller Center officials often make dozens of trips at the start of each year to search for the perfect tree, and people across the nation send pictures of trees to the center to be considered. The manager of the gardens division at the Rockefeller Center leads the year-round hunt, sometimes conducting aerial surveys from a helicopter during the winter when evergreens are more visible among rows of brown, leafless trees. These helicopter rides are followed by more focused scouting at various ground locations. Center officials

The Rockefeller Center Christmas tree is typically a Norway spruce, which can reach up to one hundred feet in height.

aim to have a tree chosen and an agreement in place by the Fourth of July of that year. Ultimately, Rockefeller Center's head gardens manager has the difficult task of making the final decision regarding tree selection. For the last 26 years, David Murbach filled this position.

Aside from the height and width requirements, there is no exact definition of a "perfect" Christmas tree. Rockefeller Center officials favor trees that are proportionate and symmetrical, with lush, dense sets of branches. Officials, and Murbach himself, must then agree that the desired tree has a unique yet indiscernible quality that sets it apart from the rest.

The 1930s

THE FIRST "OFFICIAL" Rockefeller Center Christmas tree was erected in the plaza in December of 1933 in front of the RCA Building, which had been completed just eight months prior. It measured a mere fifty feet in height, and it was decorated with seven hundred twinkling lights. Several choirs and a female trumpet trio participated in the first holiday program at the center that December. Rockefeller Center's first public relations executive, Merle Crowell, made certain that the lighting ceremony was broadcast nationally on NBC radio the following day, but otherwise, it was a small affair. Still, the size of this intimate celebration did not make it any less special. The real pomp and circumstance didn't begin until the tree of 1934 arrived at the plaza.

The seventy-foot, seven-ton Norway spruce that would become Rockefeller Center's 1934 centerpiece arrived in the center's sunken plaza early in December, having made the relatively short trek to Manhattan from Babylon, Long Island. Ceremoniously lit on December 11, this majestic tree was strung with about 1,200 multicolored lights. The festivities of 1934 also featured the first Rockefeller Center lighting ceremony

1934 featured the first lighting ceremony with musical entertainment.

to center around musical entertainment, the success of which paved the way for years of memorable and lively shows to come. The evening's musical program presented the Gloria Trumpeters, who were joined by Richard Leibert, organist at the newly completed Radio City Music Hall, and Eugene Frey, a baritone soloist in the Mendelssohn Glee Club.

Whimsical ornaments in the shapes of animals, stars, and boats dangled from the tree's branches, and a shining star perched atop the towering spruce. Four floodlights further illuminated these elegant decorations. The tree remained lit every night until 1934 melted into 1935.

The tradition continued as the United States—and New York City—began the slow process of lifting itself out of the Great Depression. In December of 1935, Rockefeller Center welcomed an eighty-foot, sixty-year-old Norway spruce, once again from Babylon, Long Island. It weighed six tons and boasted a forty-foot branch spread. Due to its great size, officials were required to obtain a special permit in order to transport it across the Queensboro Bridge. The tree was meticulously decorated with 1,700 multicolored lights, which hung on more than a mile of wiring. A sheet-metal star, illuminated with seventy lights, was placed on the tip of the magnificent tree. After the holiday season, center officials launched a recycling

In 1935, the Christmas tree was lowered into the sunken plaza by a towering crane.

campaign that would become an important part of the Rockefeller Center tradition in the 1970s: They reduced the spruce to a massive pile of firewood that was donated, log by log, to waiting fireplaces across the city.

Officials at Rockefeller Center must have felt especially extravagant in 1936 and 1937 when twin seventy-foot Norway spruces graced the center's sunken plaza during the holidays. The first pair hailed from a private estate in Morristown, New Jersey. That year has the distinction of being the first to include a skating pageant during the lighting ceremony. The Rockefeller Plaza outdoor ice skating pond had just opened, and it became an immediate success as part of the Christmas pageantry at the center. On Christmas Eve,

The Rockefeller Center Christmas tree was recycled for the first time in 1935 when it was chopped into firewood for New York families.

Oscar Richard, who, according to Rockefeller Center press releases, was the "oldest amateur fancy skater" in the country at the age of eighty-one, became the first skater to glide across the rink. The following year, a second pair of Norway spruces made the trip from the Peter Stuyvesant estate in Allamuchy, New York, to take their place of honor in the plaza.

In 1938, the center returned to its roots, dedicating its Christmas display to a single special tree. That year, a seventy-foot tree dazzled passersby with the glow of hundreds of blue lights. Topped with a large silver star, the Christmas tree sparked a color theme of blue and silver that swept all of the Christmas decorations on Rockefeller Center's grounds, as well as shop windows and displays throughout the area.

On December 14, 1939, as World War II began to escalate, a seventy-five-foot Norway spruce arrived in the plaza at Rockefeller Center. Hauled in from a New Jersey estate, the tree was the largest to stand in the center since the tradition's commencement. Dozens of workmen labored for several days to install the floodlights that would illuminate the spectacle, which was eventually decorated with hundreds of candles of varying sizes, some even reaching six feet in height! A large silver star again topped the great tree, and the lighting ceremony took place on December 18.

Decorated with countless blue bulbs and topped with a silver star, 1938's Christmas tree embodied the center's blue and silver theme that holiday season.

A crane lowered twin seventy-foot Norway spruces into the plaza in 1936 for a double dose of holiday cheer during the Christmas season.

Chapter 3

A Tradition Matures

Once the tree for the plaza has been chosen, several months of work ensue to prepare the tree for its new role as the most famous Christmas tree in America. Throughout the months leading up to November, the tree receives exceptional care, including special pruning.

By mid-November, the process of wrapping the branches, also known as *corseting*, begins. This procedure takes about a week to complete. The majority of the bottom branches are wrapped in twine and burlap to ensure the tree's delivery to New York City in the best condition possible. The branches, which are strapped to the trunk, are tightened daily to ensure that they remain closely packed together for

The head gardener counts the rings on the Christmas tree's stump to determine its age.

the trip to the Big Apple. Officials strive for a diameter of twenty to thirty feet so that the tree will be compact enough to travel on the highways and back roads that lead to the city; of course, once the branches are released again, the tree's diameter can reach up to twice that size!

After countless weeks of preparation, the actual cutting of the tree takes less than two minutes. Amid media fanfare and sometimes emotional goodbyes from the tree's owners, the evergreen is suspended using a 180-ton hydraulic crane and cut down; both handsaws and chain saws have been used to make the final chop. Once the tree has been secured on its traveling trailer, the head gardener for Rockefeller Center counts the rings on its stump to measure and record its age. After the tree has been removed, a team of gardeners stays behind to complete any necessary landscaping in the area. The donors of a tree will often request that a sapling be planted in its former place. In most cases, another Norway spruce is planted to replace the one chosen for Rockefeller Center, perhaps in the hope that it also will be showcased in New York City some day!

The 1940s

To kick off the new decade, Rockefeller Center installed an eighty-eight-foot Norway spruce in the plaza for Christmas. Arriving from the William Eastwood estate in Dutchess County, New York, it towered over the center, reaching the ninth floor of the RCA Building. It was decorated with eight hundred white plastic balls crafted

In December of 1940, seventy-two golden organ pipes graced the plaza, filling the promenade with beloved Christmas carols five times each day.

especially for the tree by Monsanto Chemical Company, and an enormous white star sat atop the highest bough. Organ music was the theme in 1940; seventy-two golden organ pipes sparkled along the Channel Gardens (the gardens between the British Empire Building and La Maison Française). Organs played classic Christmas carols throughout the lighting ceremony, and the festive music continued to play every evening during the holiday season.

Four live reindeer delighted crowds at the Rockefeller Center Christmas festivities of 1941.

The following year was a somber one as the United States declared war on Japan, officially joining the turmoil of World War II just before Christmas. More than ever, the American people needed holiday joy to lift their spirits, and in 1941, four live reindeer joined the eighty-three-foot Norway spruce—lit with eight hundred pastel red and blue bulbs— on display in the center's plaza. Raised in Lake Placid, the reindeer were brought in by the New York Zoological Society, which took full responsibility for the animals'

The first wartime Christmas trees were adorned with red, white, and blue bulbs to display patriotism, pride, and support for American troops fighting in World War II.

welfare during their stay at Rockefeller Center. The reindeer were tame enough to remain calm as crowds of people traipsed through the grounds during the holidays that year. After the new year dawned, they were sent to the Bronx Zoological Park to spend the rest of their days in a special range created especially for them. By all accounts, their presence in the center that year added a special touch to an already magical season.

The next few years brought live—rather than harvested—trees to Rockefeller Center after many New Yorkers complained about the number of trees that were cut down and thrown away every year. Rather than chopping the spruces off of their trunks, gardeners dug them out of the ground and bound their roots in burlap for their stint in the plaza. After the holidays, the trees were replanted in their homes. To support the war effort, no lights or essential war materials were used on any of the trees during these years; only small plastic decorations adorned the living branches.

In 1942, an unprecedented *three* living Norway spruce trees were brought from Huntington, Long Island, to stand on display at the center: A fifty-foot tree was erected first, flanked by a thirty-foot tree on each side. One was decorated in red, another in white, and the third in blue to commemorate the brave soldiers fighting in World War II.

A living fifty-five-foot Norway spruce was the center's focal point in 1943, and 1944 saw a sixty-five-foot living Norway spruce that hailed from an estate in West Islip, Long Island, displayed in the plaza. The Rockefeller Center Choristers held a candlelight concert beneath the tree on December 21, 1944. The Choristers, who made their caroling debut at the center in 1939, were composed of singing Rockefeller Center employees. Over the years, the group's musical ranks sometimes numbered as many as two hundred.

On December 14, 1945, the Rockefeller Center Christmas tree, a fifty-five-foot live Norway spruce from Syosset, New York, was lit with real lights for the first time since the United States had entered the war. Snow began to fall during the lighting ceremony, giving spectators an extra bit of magical holiday cheer. Robert Carson designed the lighting for that year's tree. An early example of "black light," seven hundred plastic globes painted fluorescent colors were hung from the boughs, and the tree glowed with a luminous effect when ultraviolet lights shone on its branches. After Christmas, the spruce was replanted at the estate where it had grown before making the trip to Manhattan.

In 1948, a ninety-foot Norway spruce stood at the foot of the seventy-story RCA building.

The following year welcomed another black-lit tree: a seventy-five-foot Norway spruce brought in by Syosset Nurseries in Long Island, New York. It was decorated with more than eight hundred painted globes that sparkled neon when the ultraviolet lights were aimed at them.

Discovered on a farm in Dear Park, Long Island, after months of searching, a sixty-five-foot Norway spruce graced the plaza in 1947. That year, the black light display was retired in favor of strings of clear electric lights. It was a tough decision for center officials, who noted that the black light effect had been novel and interesting, as well as energy efficient, during the war, but no significant improvements had been made in black-light technology to warrant its continued use. Now that the war had ended, they could use electric lights on the tree once again.

> *The tree was lit with real lights for the first time since the United States entered the war.*

A milestone was reached in 1948: the tallest tree to date arrived at Rockefeller Center—a ninety-foot Norway spruce from the home of Mr. and Mrs. Carl Tucker in Mount Kisco, New York. Claiming the tree for the center's Christmas display had been an exceptionally difficult task, but officials managed to bring it to the plaza . . . eventually. In 1940, center officials had approached the Tuckers about procuring their tree for that year's holiday festivities, but the Tuckers had been unwilling to part with it. Eight years later, with the tree approaching a staggering 104 years of age, they finally decided it was time for thousands of people to enjoy the spruce at Rockefeller Center. So off to Manhattan it went.

It took a dozen workmen seven hours to erect and secure the mammoth tree in Rockefeller Plaza, and thirty electricians spent several days decorating its many branches. In the end, six thousand silver and gold electric lights and eight hundred plastic snowflakes of different sizes adorned the tree, creating one of the most spectacular centerpieces in the plaza to date.

After the backbreaking work involved in the preparation of the ninety-foot tree of the previous year, 1949's seventy-five-footer was a welcome respite. The Norway spruce from Yaphank, New York, was painted wintry silver-white using two hundred gallons of fireproof paint.

Workers decorate the topmost branches of the tree while it is still lying in a horizontal position, before it is erected in the plaza.

Chapter 4

TRADITION AND PROSPERITY

nce the tree is selected, prepared, trussed, and removed from its home, a team of fifteen to twenty people uses a hydraulic crane to hoist it onto a custom telescoping trailer. This trailer can stretch to one hundred feet in length, and it can hold a tree as tall as 125 feet. (Sometimes special accommodations have been made for longer trips, or for when transporting the tree on the water has been more convenient!) A plastic solution is sometimes sprayed on the branches of the tree to keep them green throughout the holiday season.

The soon-to-be Christmas tree then travels to New York City escorted by police cars, usually in the middle of the night so that it doesn't disrupt traffic too much. The trailer makes use of roads and bridges as much as possible because it cannot fit through tunnels given the size of its cargo. When the heavily guarded—and paparazzi-flanked—tree arrives in Rockefeller Center just before dawn, the same hydraulic crane that lifted it from its trunk is used to position it in its place of honor at the center of Rockefeller Plaza.

It usually takes about one full day to install the tree in the center, and it can take several weeks more to decorate and prepare the spruce for the lighting ceremony of early December. After that, the tree doesn't require as much maintenance as one may think during its time on display for the millions of people who visit it during the Christmas season. It is generally lit every evening until the first week of January, and, as long as the wind doesn't knock down the decorations, it is left alone to stand majestically in the plaza.

Surprisingly, the tree doesn't even need water! This may sound implausible, but the tree is never watered once it is standing in Rockefeller Center. Even though conventional practice mandates that we add water to our Christmas trees at home every day, the difference is that we artificially heat our homes during the winter months, which dries out the tree. This heat is not available in the outdoor plaza at Rockefeller Center (though some ice skaters and shoppers might wish it were on a particularly frigid day in December!). The cold climate allows the giant tree to retain its water throughout the weeks leading up to Christmas, and the occasional rain or snow shower helps, too.

The Norway spruce has become a celebrated symbol of Christmastime.

The 1950s

THE CHRISTMAS TREE that helped usher in a new, prosperous decade in the United States was set up in pouring rain in early December of 1950. Weighing ten tons, the eighty-five-foot Norway spruce from Hollingsworth Wood estate in Mount Kisco, New York, was eventually strung with eight thousand lights.

An eighty-two-foot Norway spruce was chosen to be the center's tree in 1951; it was brought to the city from the Syosset Nursery in Lake Ronkonkoma, Long Island, and took nearly seven hours to set up once it reached the plaza after a fifty-mile ride. That year's theme was "Christmas gardens." The promenade was lined with rows of blue-lit fountains. Blue, green, and white plastic bubbles rested on these fountains, surrounded by luminous stars. That year was the first to see the Rockefeller Center tree lit on national television, and it was the perfect year for it. The plaza was truly resplendent: the tree glowed with ten thousand lights of various colors, and the gardens were decorated to resemble a winter wonderland.

The tradition of the Norway spruce continued through the early 1950s, with an eighty-five-footer from the Peter Stuyvesant estate in Allamuchy, New York, coming to the

The Christmas garden theme of 1951, complete with simulated fountains, extended from Fifth Avenue to the lower plaza of Rockefeller Center, creating a pathway to the majestic Christmas tree.

center in 1952. Actress Kate Smith had the distinct honor of lighting this evergreen on December 12, 1952, as thousands of spectators looked on in wonder. The lighting design was truly inspired. It included hundreds of yellow, white, and red globe lights, as well as five thousand white fairy lights. More than three hundred towering gold and white candles

Twelve herald angels designed by Valerie Clarebout graced the plaza in 1952, and the beautiful sculptures soon became a part of the Rockefeller Center Christmas tradition.

illuminated the Channel Gardens. The ceremony featured a concert by the Rockefeller Center Choristers, who continued to sing in the plaza throughout the holiday season. Organ music filled the center during daily concerts at lunchtime, and carol programs were a great success every evening.

A slightly smaller—but no less magnificent—seventy-five-foot tree donated by William P. Jenks made the journey from Morristown, New Jersey, in 1953 to become the center's main attraction. Its trunk was three and a half feet thick, and workers used a powerful chain saw to cut through it, which was no small feat.

Belvidere, New Jersey, had the honor of supplying Norway spruce trees for the Christmas celebrations of 1954 and 1955. A sixty-five-year-old, sixty-five-foot specimen was trailer-trucked to Rockefeller Plaza on the morning of November 29, 1954, from the estate of Elmer Rowe in Belvidere. The Channel Gardens were decorated with wire-sculpted angels by English sculptor Valerie Clarebout, and the fountains were filled with evergreens. The tree was trimmed with two thousand multicolored electric lights, and a plastic four-foot star perched on the top. The lighting ceremony took place on December 9, and the tree remained lit every evening thereafter until it was taken down on January 2. Belvidere was the proud supplier of another sixty-five-foot Norway spruce to serve as 1955's Christmas tree. That holiday season, there was a candlelight chorale concert in Rockefeller Center on Tuesday and Wednesday evenings at dusk.

The year 1956 ushered in a trend of white spruces that lasted for three consecutive holiday seasons. The first of the white spruces, a sixty-four-foot, sixty-five-year-old tree, was from Charles W. Elliott's dairy farm in Whitefield, New Hampshire. The state's governor, Lane Dwinell, donated it to Rockefeller Center as a gift. Its journey to Manhattan spanned five states, totaling 335 miles: the longest trip a Rockefeller Center Christmas tree had made up to that point. Unfortunately, the trip was a bit hard on the spruce. Once it was erected in the plaza, workmen had to reattach dozens of branches that had fallen off in the process of raising the tree into place.

The next two years also saw white spruce trees take the place of honor in Rockefeller Center during the Christmas season. Mr. and Mrs. Maurice Plante of Island Pond, Vermont, donated 1957's sixty-five-footer. Several boys who had been camping in the area had spotted the tree that summer, and officials from the Vermont Forestry and Park departments had offered it to grateful Rockefeller Center officials. The tree was not easy to retrieve: A road had to be bulldozed to reach the coveted spruce, but it was worth it.

The *Today* show interviewed the Plante family along with Vermont Governor Joseph B. Johnson in Island Pond at a send-off ceremony. Formal celebrations such as this would be common in years to come, especially when trees were selected from small towns to become the most famous Christmas trees in the country. The small hamlet of Island Pond is situated very close to the Canadian border, and the tree made the lengthy 375-mile trip to New York City escorted by police. To make way for the enormous tree to take its place in the plaza, the eighty-one United Nations flags that line Rockefeller Center were temporarily removed.

This was the most extensive search for a tree yet, and the coveted evergreen made for another breathtaking display in the plaza that December.

The Plantes' tree was lit December 12, 1957, in a ceremony attended by Mr. and Mrs. Plante and their three children, who made their first trip to Manhattan to watch their tree become famous. Governor Johnson hosted the ceremony, in which more than one thousand lantern-type

In 1959, another magnificent evergreen became the plaza's Christmas centerpiece.

lights and another three thousand fairy lights were ignited to illuminate the towering evergreen.

A sixty-four-foot spruce from East Madison, Maine, briefly took residence in Rockefeller Plaza in 1958. In April of that year, Maine Governor Edmund S. Muskie had been told that center officials wanted a tree from his state, and several months of difficult searching by Maine Forestry

Department wardens had finally yielded the beautiful tree that traveled down the eastern seaboard in November of that year. The spruce's trek from Maine to Manhattan became the longest journey a Christmas tree had made to Rockefeller Center, unseating the New Hampshire tree of two years prior.

In 1959, a seventy-foot, eighty-year-old Norway spruce from Podunk, Massachusetts stood proudly in Rockefeller Plaza. Harold O. Cook, the oldest living forester in the United States at the time, made a gift of the tree to Rockefeller Center after a statewide hunt by the Massachusetts Department of Natural Resources that lasted for several months. They finally found the tree on the property of Alva Silliman in Podunk, and the spruce was felled amidst heavy rains on a Saturday in late November. It made the long trip to Manhattan in the rain and snow, and twenty men spent an entire week erecting scaffolding and decorating the three-ton evergreen.

This was the most extensive search for a tree yet, and the coveted evergreen made for another breathtaking display in the plaza that December. Lit on December 10 of that year, the tree's stunning beauty made the arduous search worth every moment.

The Swarovski crystal star has become a significant part of the Rockefeller Center Christmas tree tradition, pictured perched atop the tree of 2004.

Chapter 5

KEEPING UP WITH TRADITION

Decorating a tree that is several stories high is no small task—imagine how much more work goes into trimming a ninety-foot evergreen! Before the tree is set vertically in the plaza, it remains on its trailer, where workmen decorate the topmost branches with wiring, lights, and sometimes ornaments (in recent years, though, the decorations have been limited to only lights and a star on the top). Carpenters drill a steel rod into the trunk, which keeps the tree secured in its base, and the star is fastened firmly in place at the tip of the tree.

Although many different types of ornaments have graced Rockefeller Center Christmas trees over the years, a star is *always* the topper. From the 1940s through the 1990s and into the early twenty-first century, a creative team at the center crafted a four-foot plastic star for the tree. In 2004, a nine-foot-wide, 550-pound Swarovski crystal star replaced the plastic one on the uppermost bough of the tree. It sparkled with twenty-five thousand crystals, and in 2005, L.E.D. lights were added to enhance the glow.

Once the star is in place, the Christmas tree is raised into a vertical position and secured. Next, it's time to construct the scaffolding that will hold the dozens of electricians who will spend the next few days wrapping every branch with miles of wire for the lights. Through the years, electric lights have been most frequently chosen as decoration for the tree, with brief suspensions during World War II and the energy crisis in the early 1970s. The mid-1940s saw black lights used for the first time on the tree, and sometimes only white lights have graced its boughs. Throughout the tradition's history, themes for the tree have included snowflakes, large colored globes, bells, gold adornments, blue-and-silver ornaments, animals, candles, and even pipe organs. Now, the Rockefeller Center Christmas tree is decorated only with multicolored lights and the Swarovski star.

The Channel Gardens must also be decorated for Christmas every year, and they have featured many memorably beautiful displays. Perhaps the loveliest, and certainly the most popular,

Thousands of multicolor lights glimmer on the boughs of the Rockefeller Center Christmas tree.

are the aluminum wire angels created by British sculptor Valerie Clarebout. The twelve figures were first displayed at the center in 1954, and every year for the past twenty, the herald angels have been refurbished and displayed in their rightful place in the Channel Gardens.

The 1960s

A CHRISTMAS CONTROVERSY kicked off the 1960s in Rockefeller Center. Rockefeller Center Christmas tree scouts selected a tree for 1960 that had captured their interest about ten years earlier: a sixty-five-foot Norway spruce growing in front of the home of Mr. and Mrs. Emanuel Owens in North Harford in Susquehanna County, Pennsylvania. The Owenses had initially refused to donate their tree because of its small size; however, by 1960, the evergreen had grown so large that it almost completely obstructed their view of the lake across from their home. If the tree fell, it would destroy their house (and besides, they were interested in building a garage in the tree's place!). Center officials offered four hundred dollars for the spruce, and the Owenses finally accepted the offer. With the tree chosen and the deal secured, everything should have run smoothly as it had in the past, but there was more controversy still to come.

Rockefeller Center officials were preparing the Owenses' tree for its New York City debut when a reporter for the *Philadelphia Inquirer* decided to take on the century-old tree as his cause. Columnist John M. Cummings wrote a letter to Pennsylvania Governor David L. Lawrence begging him to intervene on the tree's behalf. He even sent a twenty-five dollar

In 1960, a choir of Korean orphans performed at the base of the Christmas tree in Rockefeller Plaza.

check in hopes that the governor would start a fund to save the tree. Ultimately, though, because the tree belonged to the Owens family, legally they had the power to stand by their agreement with Rockefeller Center. They sent their spruce to Manhattan despite the columnist's objections.

No such drama befell the tree preparations in 1961, when an eighty-five-foot Norway spruce from the home of Mr. and Mrs. M.A. Gilmartin Jr. of Smithtown, New York, made its home in the plaza of Rockefeller Center during the Christmas season. At the lighting ceremony, the St. Thomas Protestant Episcopal Church choir sang carols as Laurance S. Rockefeller, John D. Rockefeller Jr.'s son and chairman of Rockefeller Center, pushed the button to illuminate the tree's four thousand sparkling electric lights, representing the unofficial start of the national holiday season.

Laurance Rockefeller again had the honor of lighting the sixty-seven-foot white spruce, a gift from the Scott Paper Company, at the 1962 ceremony. Its five-hundred-mile journey from Greenville Junction, Maine, set another record as the longest trip a tree had yet made to New York City.

Dr. and Mrs. Elbert H. Loughran of Hurley, New York, donated their sixty-foot Norway spruce to Rockefeller Center in 1963. The tree experts at the center had been searching for six months when they received a picture in the mail from the Loughrans, who were starting to worry that the magnificent tree might fall on their home. Dr. Loughran's father had planted it as a seedling in 1910, and more than a half-century later, the thirty-six-foot branch spread had begun to look menacing. The Loughrans were offered one hundred dollars for their tree, and they donated that small honorarium to the Kingston Hospital Building Fund. Their spruce arrived in Rockefeller Plaza on December 2, and it was lit during a ceremony on December 12 after ten arduous days of full-time decorating.

Another sixty-footer traveled to Rockefeller Center to become the nation's most beloved Christmas tree in 1964. This Norway spruce hailed from the home of Mr. and Mrs. Vito D'Auria in Lake Carmel, New York. It was a good year for the Rockefeller Center tree scouts—they found the sixty-year-old beauty early, in July! By 1965, yet another sixty-foot Norway spruce made the trip to the plaza. Mr. and Mrs. Charles Fagg of Darien, Connecticut, contributed their tree, which has the distinction of being the first tree in the center's history to come from the Nutmeg State.

A white spruce from Petawawa Forest in Canada has the noteworthy honor of being the only Rockefeller Center Christmas tree to have ever come from outside of the United

> *It had that "special something," that immeasurable, Christmas-tree quality that scouts from Rockefeller Center long to find.*

States. In 1966, the sixty-four-foot tree, which grew up 120 miles north of Ottawa, was a gift to the center from the Canadian government in celebration of Canada's centennial the following year. The evergreen traveled 550 miles to get to New York City, the longest trip to date for a Rockefeller Center tree. The year of 1966 carries another distinction: record high temperatures throughout the Christmas season. On the day of the lighting ceremony, December 9, temperatures

In honor of their centennial in 1967, Canada presented Rockefeller Center with a sixty-four foot white spruce.

rose to a whopping sixty-six degrees in New York! Despite the unusually warm weather, skaters and shoppers still felt the holiday spirit as the giant tree was illuminated . . . even though they weren't in a typical winter wonderland.

Thirty-four years after the first building in Rockefeller Center opened—and after the first official tree was erected in the plaza—another balsam fir was put in the place of honor as the center's Christmas tree. The tree of 1967 was sixty-five feet tall, quite a bit bigger than 1931's "unofficial" twenty-foot balsam. It journeyed from Coventry, Vermont, and sparkled beautifully throughout the season, much as the following year's fifty-five-foot white spruce did. Another New England tree, 1958's spruce journeyed from Holland, Vermont.

To bring the decade to a close, a seventy-foot balsam fir stood proudly over Rockefeller Center throughout the Christmas season. After months of searching for just the right tree, officials had found the perfect candidate in Saranac Lake, New York. Its branch spread measured thirty-three feet, it was about sixty-five years old, and it weighed more than three tons. But it also had that "special something," that immeasurable, Christmas-tree quality that scouts from Rockefeller Center long to find.

The search for the perfect Christmas
tree can take months.

Chapter 6

TRADITION GOES GREEN

The 1970s saw the first step in a turn toward greener trees—but not in color. With the exception of 1935's tree, which was chopped into small logs and distributed to residents of New York City for use as firewood, most of Rockefeller Center's trees were simply taken down and thrown away. By the 1970s, as people were becoming more conscious of their environment and conservation, this had become an issue. People across the nation began to protest the practice of chopping down trees for use at Christmas time, only to dispose of them at the holiday's end. There had to be a better way.

Everyone seemed to have a suggestion for the Rockefeller Center Christmas tree: Keep the tree alive and plant it in Central Park after Christmas. Chop it up and use it for building. Replant it in its home. Make it into mulch.

In 1971, a new tradition was born: the Christmas tree was chipped and turned into mulch—three tons of it! Since that time, it has become a custom to recycle the gargantuan Rockefeller Center tree after each Christmas.

Usually, the largest portion of the trunk is made into a horse jump for the United States Equestrian Team at their course in Gladstone, New Jersey. The tons of mulch that are produced from each tree are given to Boy Scout camps or New York City parks for use on trails. One year, the spruce was cut into planks and used to build an addition onto the home of the people who had originally owned the tree. Officials donated another tree to Habitat for Humanity for use in building projects all over the world. Another year, the Christmas tree's scraps were taken to the Central Park Zoo, where goats, monkeys, otters, and even polar bears enjoyed the tree's remains in their respective habitats. There was even a Christmas tree that was hand crafted into the mast of a great sailing ship!

Another ecological concern arose unexpectedly in the 1970s: the energy crisis precipitated by the oil embargo of 1973 and 1974. As a result, 1973's tree glittered with fewer lights than usual. As environmental issues have continued to gain prominence in our national conscience, other modifications to the tradition involving the Rockefeller Center Christmas tree have arisen.

Polar bears, among other animals, benefitted from recycled Rockefeller Center Christmas trees in their habitats in the Central Park Zoo.

The most major change occurred in 2007, when, for the first time, the tree was lit entirely with thirty thousand L.E.D. lights. L.E.D. stands for "light-emitting diodes," tiny bulbs that fit into an electrical circuit. They have no filaments that burn out, so they last longer. Because they don't need to warm up in order to glow, they don't produce any heat, and they are energy efficient. The lights on 2007's Christmas tree were powered exclusively by 365 solar panels that topped the buildings at 45 Rockefeller Plaza, and this modification saved a great amount of power—as much as the average family uses in a month!

The Rockefeller Center Christmas tree tradition turned "green" during the 1970s.

The 1970s

A SIXTY-FOOT WHITE SPRUCE from Coventry, Vermont, was set up in Rockefeller Plaza to welcome the new decade, and another Vermont tree took the place of honor in 1971. A sixty-five-foot balsam fir from the Robert Bragg family farm in East Montpelier, the tree has the distinction of being the first to be recycled at the end of the holiday season. A spectacular lighting ceremony took place that year, featuring musical performances by the All-City High School Choir and Metropolitan Opera singer William Walker, among others. Five children from the Bragg family and fifteen Cub Scouts from Brooklyn stood beneath the tree and triggered its illumination on December 9, 1971.

The next two years saw sixty-five-foot Norway spruce trees take up residence in the plaza for Christmas. Old Bridge, New Jersey, was the birthplace of 1972's spruce, while the tree for 1973's Christmas celebration traced its roots to Tenafly, New Jersey. During the energy crisis that year, fewer lights were used to illuminate the great spruce, though it still shone brightly and brought joy to millions of people.

In 1974, a Norway spruce of sixty-three feet in height became the most celebrated Christmas tree in the nation. It was donated to Rockefeller Center from Lehighton, Pennsylvania. Perhaps more noteworthy, though, was the 1974 premier of "TubaChristmas." For several years at Christmastime in Rockefeller Plaza, hundreds of tuba players converged, playing Christmas carols and making merry throughout Midtown Manhattan. It was quite a unique sight to see.

Jean Wolfe saw her tree glow with holiday spirit at Rockefeller Center in 1975. A small crowd of sentimental towns-people gathered to bid the fifty-nine-foot balsam fir adieu in New Canaan, Connecticut, on November 20 of that year. Planted in the late 1920s, the tree had been beloved by the neighborhood children who climbed its trunk and built forts in its sturdy branches. It was an emotional goodbye for the people of New Canaan. Like all of its predecessors, Wolfe's tree became a monument to Christmas, decorated with multicolored globe lights and illuminated on December 4.

In 1976, Florence and Edward Praisner from Montclair, New Jersey, donated their sixty-eight-foot Norway spruce to the center for its bicentennial Christmas celebration. It was not an easy decision for Florence Praisner, whose mother had used the live tree as her Christmas tree in 1927. After the holiday season, the tree had been planted in her front yard, where it had been maturing since. The couple looked on their tree with sentimentality, but, like many owners of enormous trees, they were beginning to worry that the tree's age—in combination with the weather—was not on their side. They feared that a hurricane would topple the tree, destroying their home. They discussed their worries with their son, who contacted Rockefeller Center.

That year, Rockefeller Center officials received dozens of solicitations from owners who wanted to see their majestic trees become the Christmas tree. After examining the Praisners' tree, officials decided that it was perfect and

Spectators enjoyed Rockefeller Center's bicentennial Christmas celebration in 1976.

ended the year's search. The spruce weighed three and a half tons and had a width of thirty feet at its widest point, with full, lush branches. Soon those branches were being wrapped with lights strung upon miles—and miles—of wiring at Rockefeller Center. After about ten days of work, the tree was ready for its illumination ceremony on December 9, 1976. The Praisners, along with their three sons and their families, traveled to Manhattan to watch their old spruce spark Christmas joy in Manhattan. For one of the Praisners' sons, though, it was not an easy trip. He'd loved the tree since he was a young boy, and he had a difficult time saying goodbye; however, as soon as he saw its beauty shining in the plaza, he knew that his family had made the right decision.

Other parts of the city—and the country—were beginning to replicate the joy created by the Rockefeller Center Christmas tree tradition by decorating large public trees of their own.

A sixty-five-foot white spruce that had grown in Dixfield, Maine, became 1977's Rockefeller Center Christmas tree and the third Christmas tree to come from the great state of Maine. The Immaculate Conception Seminary in

Mahwah, New Jersey, donated the tree in 1978: a seventy-five-foot Norway spruce. By this time, other parts of the city—and the country—were beginning to replicate the joy created by the Rockefeller Center Christmas tree tradition by decorating large public trees of their own. That year, Harlem erected its first giant Christmas tree.

The last Christmas tree to grace the center in the 1970's was a sixty-five-foot Norway spruce from Spring Valley, New York, but the new decade did not enter without incident. The tree was put up and lit with fanfare as always, and holiday celebrations ensued with no remarkable occurrences until December 27, 1979, when a man named George Young climbed the tree in Rockefeller Center.

At that time, fifty-two American diplomats had been held hostage in Iran since November 4 of that year, and Young, a twenty-seven-year-old, and his friend Thomas Kijewski, who was twenty-four, climbed the tree in protest. Another friend of the two men, Dennis Matinet, a nineteen-year-old from Brooklyn, had shoved a guard aside, allowing the bold pair to scale the fence around the tree and attempt to climb it. Young remained at the top of the tree for nearly an hour and a half, yelling, "Free the fifty!" Kijewski, though, returned to the ground in obedience to the orders of a Rockefeller Center security guard (after climbing only twelve feet up the trunk).

Young was eventually coaxed down by center officials, who assured him that his protest would not lead to the freeing of the hostages at the United States embassy in Tehran. He was cited for trespassing. The fifty-two hostages were eventually set free, but not until January 20, 1981, giving another young man ample time to climb the following year's tree soon after the lighting ceremony.

Chapter 7

MEN OF TRADITION

Think Martha Stewart has the market cornered on all things Christmas tree-related? Think again. Carl Miller, David Murbach, and Anthony Ciufo could show her a thing or two.

It takes a particular kind of person to spend months and months out of every year thinking about Christmas and searching for the perfect tree. And it takes a fair amount of people power—and specialized equipment—to realize the spectacle of the Rockefeller Center Christmas tree each year.

Carl Miller, vice president of operations at the center, was in charge of choosing the tree in the late 1970s and early 1980s. He was incredibly selective because he'd hear from New Yorkers who weren't too shy to voice their complaints when they weren't pleased with a year's tree.

Driving through the countryside of New York, New Jersey, Pennsylvania, and Connecticut in the spring to search for a Christmas tree in sparsely populated areas, Miller often piqued the curiosity of the few people who spotted him. The locals were sometimes skeptical when they heard the reason for the unfamiliar vehicle slowly winding its way through their otherwise quiet neighborhoods: "I want to make your tree famous!" was not a statement they heard every day.

The search for the perfect Christmas tree can be arduous, and once a tree is found, there's no guarantee that its owners will hand it over willingly. More often than not, Miller had to cajole a tree's owners and devotees into donat-

In 1985, rainstorms created enough mud to hamper the process of removing that year's Christmas tree from its home.

Millions of spectators enjoy the Rockefeller Center Christmas tree every year.

ing it. Then, of course, there's the matter of removing the tree and carting it the great distance to Rockefeller Center.

For this task, the center has worked with Torsilieri Inc., a Gladstone, New Jersey, landscaping business founded by the Torsilieri family in 1968. Torsilieri began its stint as the transporter of the most famous Christmas trees in America in 1982, and this company has worked with center officials since that time to procure and move the desired evergreens.

Murbach graduated from the University of Arizona with a degree in forestry, and he received a master's degree from the University of Delaware in public garden administration. He then became a horticulturist and the manager of the gardens at Rockefeller Center. He spent nine months in 1999 and 2000 as a Loeb fellow at Harvard University conducting an environment-related independent study, and then began dividing his time between New York City and West Palm Beach, Florida, where he managed the Horticulture Society of South Florida. The American Association of Botanical Gardens and Arboreta awarded him a citation in 1994, and the Horticultural Society of New York honored him in 1999. Murbach's job involved much more than the search for a single tree, though. He oversaw several floral exhibits throughout the year, as well as a large-scale flower show, and he rotated the landscaped exhibitions in the Channel Gardens seasonally. Still, his position as the chief scout for the Rockefeller Center Christmas tree was clearly his claim to fame, and he did not take the job lightly. Every year, he searched diligently for the perfect tree, spending days on end with nothing but Christmas on his mind, regardless of the season. In 1997, Murbach told The New York Times that he looked for trees with "personality." Perhaps this, to him, is that "special something."

The Rockefeller Center employee who likely feels the most like Ebenezer Scrooge is he who takes down the Christmas tree in early January every year. Throughout the 1970s and 1980s, that man was Anthony Ciufo, a New Jersey landscaper in charge of the tree's removal. The process that takes months of preparation, followed by weeks of transportation and decoration, requires only about six hours to reverse. The thousands of lights are carefully removed from each bough after the tree has been lowered into a horizontal position by a crane. Workers then remove the branches and chop the trunk into pieces, which are recycled for use in a variety of ways, from horse jumps to trail mulch.

The 1980s

The Me Decade of the 1980s kicked off in Rockefeller Center with a win-win proposition from a retired AT&T executive in Suffern, New York, who called Carl Miller early in the year to offer him a tree that was in the way of his greenhouse. Miller traveled to the country to investigate, and he found that the executive's tree had a split trunk, which made it unusable for Christmas; however, while he was there, another tree caught Miller's attention. To Miller, the sixty-five-foot Norway spruce with full boughs looked perfect. A deal was struck wherein Miller's crew removed the tree that blocked the greenhouse, and, in return, they were given the ideal Christmas tree for that year's display. In an unusual turn of events, Charles Mapes, after his initial call to Miller, would provide two more trees to be used at Christmastime in Rockefeller Center, one in 1987 and another in 1991.

Another surprising incident marked the Christmas of 1980: Following the protestors of the previous year, another man climbed the Rockefeller Center Christmas tree. Anthony Philips scaled the spruce on December 9, 1980, just after it was lit that evening in front of thousands of people. Although Philips made no public statement regarding his reasons for climbing to the top of the Christmas tree, the nineteen-year-old from the Bronx was presumed to have been protesting the continued hostage situation in Iran, just as George Young had done. When he returned to the ground, Philips turned himself in to police. He was charged with criminal trespassing, disorderly conduct, resisting arrest, and reckless endangerment. Two other men who were cheering him on were also arrested and charged with disorderly conduct.

Things had calmed down by 1981, when a sixty-five-foot white spruce from the small town of West Danville, Vermont, came to be the center's symbol of Christmas. Robert Williams, a landscaper and tree harvester who had scouted trees for Rockefeller Center in the past, had nurtured the evergreen since 1979. Williams notified center officials, who examined and approved the spruce earlier in the year. B&E Landscape Company and Giberson Tree Service, both New Jersey companies, took care of the corseting, cutting, and transporting, eventually escorting the towering spruce on its twenty-hour trip to the Big Apple.

In 1982, the Immaculate Conception Seminary in Mahwah, New Jersey, donated a seventy-foot Norway spruce to Rockefeller Center. The same institution had also donated 1978's tree. A seventy-five-foot Norway spruce from Valley Cottage, New York, took the place of honor in Rockefeller Plaza in 1983. Donated by Mr. and Mrs. Allan Heinsohn, the tree weighed three tons and had a thirty-five-foot branch spread. During its lighting ceremony, Leslie Uggams and Hal Linden headlined the musical and dancing program. After Christmas that year, the tree was mulched into ground cover for a Boy Scout Council campsite in northern New Jersey.

The year 1984 saw another seventy-five-foot Norway spruce make a temporary home in Rockefeller Center. A two-ton beauty from Far Hills, New Jersey, the spruce made the journey to New York City on November 16 to prepare for its lighting ceremony on December 3.

Richard and Diane Dohl of Harveyville, Pennsylvania, donated a seventy-five-foot Norway spruce to the center in 1985; however, on November 22, 1985, early morning snow became early morning rain, which turned the grounds in the tree's pasture to mud. The tractor-trailer got stuck during the process of loading the tree from the Dohls' cattle farm, delaying the early arrival of Christmas in New York. It took all day and much of the evening to pull the crane out of the mud using a bulldozer. Because wide loads were prohibited at night on Pennsylvania state roads, the transport team had to wait until the following day to ride into Manhattan. Christmas festivities still came; they were just a day late.

In 1986, Rockefeller Center officials already had their eye on a particular tree. They inquired of the owners if the tree could become the focal point of the Rockefeller Center Christmas celebrations, but, in a family vote, the owners' seven-year-old daughter turned them down.

Rockefeller Center officials had to look elsewhere. They eventually discovered a sixty-eight-foot Norway spruce on the grounds of Mary and Vinnie Froeling's property in Nanuet, New York.

Charles Mapes, the retired executive from Suffern, New York, who gave up 1980's beautiful sixty-five-foot Norway spruce for center officials, again became involved in the tradition when he donated the tree that was decorated and admired in Rockefeller Center in 1987. This time, he made a gift of a seventy-five-foot Norway spruce from his forty-six acre property, cementing his reputation as a great source of Rockefeller Center Christmas trees.

The following two years closed out the 1980s with Norway spruce trees: 1988's tree was a seventy-five-footer donated by Rich and Lynn Luster from their home in Raritan Township, New Jersey, while John Myers gave the center a seventy-foot specimen from his property in 1989. Both made a splendid sight, their towering branches twinkling with thousands of multicolored lights throughout the holiday season and into the next year, the second adding to the celebration when New Yorkers rang in a new decade—the 1990s.

Another magnificent evergreen towered over the sunken plaza in 1998.

Chapter 8

Tradition in the Modern Era

The four-block area between 47th and 51st streets and from Fifth Avenue to Sixth has a rich, fascinating history. The land's original Dutch inhabitants would likely have been stunned to see today's Art Deco commercial complex of Rockefeller Center.

Paul Manship's golden statue of Prometheus and the enormous seventy-story skyscraper at 30 Rockefeller Center—the RCA Building—are icons of New York City, images that everyone knows whether he's visited Manhattan or not. Also among New York's icons is the Rockefeller family, with its generations of powerful and prominent businessmen. Although the Rockefeller family no longer owns Rockefeller Center, it remains a beloved Midtown landmark as iconic as the family itself.

The Rockefeller family has become an icon of New York City [from left to right: Mrs. J.D. Rockefeller Jr., D.M. Milton and his wife, and Mr. J.D. Rockefeller Jr.].

David Rockefeller is the youngest son of John D. Rockefeller Jr., without whose vision and tenacity Rockefeller Center never would have been built. David became chairman of Rockefeller Group Inc. in 1982, and he was actively involved in the center's activities throughout the 1980s into the 1990s. He participated in plans to improve and modernize the center during this time, but in September of 1989, he and his associates sold eighty percent of their interest in Rockefeller Center to the Japanese Mitsubishi Estate Corporation.

The sale was met with controversy and anger from many throughout New York and the nation. Pontiac car manufacturers ran ads on television that year that stated: "Let's go see the tree at Hirohito Center!" This sparked a fair amount of uproar among Americans. Media pundits and ordinary citizens needn't have worried about the Japanese taking over a cherished New York landmark, though; in 1995, in the wake of the real estate market collapsing, Rockefeller Center—and its Japanese investors—went bankrupt.

David Rockefeller immediately returned to save his family's business. In 1996, he assembled a group of investors to buy back the center. The recession ended, the center was refurbished, and by the holiday season of 2000, Rockefeller Center was sold for $1.85 million to another investor group, now known as Tishman Speyer, which still owns the center today. While no one named Rockefeller owns any part of Rockefeller Center, David Rockefeller is still a minority partner in the investor group.

Tishman Speyer is a real estate development firm that was founded by Jerry Speyer and Robert Tishman in 1978. The firm owns several other famed New York City landmarks besides Rockefeller Center, including the Chrysler Building and the skyscraper that houses the New York Times on Forty-third Street. Still, Tishman Speyer keeps its headquarters in Rockefeller Plaza, all the better to oversee the rich tradition of the Christmas tree that has been nurtured there since the 1930s.

The 1990s

TO KICK OFF THIS NEW DECADE of big changes for Rockefeller Center, David Murbach, the gardens manager, selected a stunning seventy-five-foot Norway spruce from the grounds of Shirley Cenci's home in West Norwalk, Connecticut, to be 1990's main attraction during the Christmas season.

The most dependable tree donor in Rockefeller Center's history, Charles Mapes of Suffern, New York, presented a third tree to the center in 1991: a stunning Norway spruce that measured sixty-five feet in height and forty-four feet at its widest point. It weighed twelve tons and was almost seventy years old. The evergreen took two weeks to be trimmed, prepped, and decorated with more than twenty-five thousand lights on wires that stretched for five miles.

In 1992, the center proudly erected a sixty-five-foot Norway spruce donated by Andrew Kupusinkis in Stony Point, New York, and 1993 saw another New York tree make a monumental stand in Rockefeller Plaza. This one, though, had been spotted two years before, in the winter of 1991, as David Murbach surveyed the area from the bird's-eye view of a helicopter. It took nearly an entire year to get in touch with Ray and Marie Cronin, who owned the property in Nanuet, New York, where the Norway spruce was growing beside their garage. Because this wasn't the Cronins' primary residence (they were renting out the house at the time), contacting the family proved difficult. When officials finally managed to contact them, the Cronins were thrilled to donate their eighty-five-foot, ten-ton tree to the Christmas spectacular at Rockefeller Center. The spruce

Dozens of workers spend countless hours decorating the Christmas tree and preparing the evergreen for its debut in Rockefeller Center.

was beautifully lit with twenty-seven thousand lights on five miles of wiring that year, and it made for quite an impressive sight standing tall in the plaza.

Maria and Alan Eglar donated 1994's Christmas tree: an eighty-five-foot Norway spruce that had been growing on their Ridgefield, Connecticut, property for seventy years. The Eglars had begun to worry that the massive evergreen would fall on their house someday, and they mailed a photograph of the tree to Rockefeller Center. While Rockefeller Center officials rarely respond to individual photographs,

Murbach snatched the elegant beauty, brought it to the center, and ordered that a sapling be planted in its place. On December 2 of that year, the tree glittered with twenty-five thousand lights on another five miles of wire, marking another breathtaking start to the Christmas season in New York City.

The Rockefeller Center Christmas tree of 1995 remains one of the most famous trees in the center's history. The tree that would eventually stand tall on the plaza that year was actually spied eleven years earlier as Guy Torsilieri (of the Torsilieri landscaping firm that transports the trees to Manhattan every year) was driving through Mendham, New Jersey, in rural Morris County. He spotted the towering Norway spruce by the Mallinckrodt Convent, an elegant brick building surrounded by acres of equally well-maintained grounds. The tree was perfect.

However, when Torsilieri returned with center officials to make a pitch to the Sisters of Christian Charity, the women unequivocally declined. One of the head nuns, Sister Marion Utz, told the officials that they would never give away the tree, regardless of the circumstances. Center officials respected her decision and selected a different tree—a Norway spruce from nearby Far Hills, New Jersey—in

1984. Still, Rockefeller Center employees did not refrain from making entreaties almost yearly to the nuns at Mallinckrodt, whom they were certain would eventually relent and donate the prized tree.

The convent itself is rather unique, as well. About sixty nuns live there full-time, with others coming and going depending on missions. The sisters also run a two-year college on the property. As the years passed, Rockefeller Center officials continued to woo the Sisters of Christian Charity, hoping they might eventually be convinced to part with their beloved tree. For the first time in the tradition's history, scouts made multiple return trips to Mendham in attempts to obtain this particular tree, which, despite the obstacles in their way, they refused to give up.

Ultimately, the irrevocable forces of nature sided with Rockefeller Center. Several difficult winters caused a few trees on the convent grounds to fall, which began to make the nuns nervous. The coveted tree continued to both age and grow remarkably tall, making it vulnerable to tree rot and other ailments. It also stood beside the front door to the convent, a rather precarious position. So, in January of 1995, at the behest of science teacher Sister Cletus Waldman—who warned that this special tree might fall and crush them all—Sister Marion Utz relented. She called the center and told David Murbach that he could finally have the tree.

By this time, the tree was seventy-five feet tall and sixty-three years old, having been planted with several other saplings in 1931—the same year, coincidentally, that Rockefeller Center had its first Christmas tree. It had grown up with many of the nuns who lived at the convent, and they treasured it as a member of their family. Throughout the winter, spring, and summer of 1995, the nuns lovingly took care of their tree until the time came to corset the branches and prepare it for its journey to Manhattan. In early November, the sisters held a ceremony and blessed the tree, reciting a prayer and sprinkling holy water on its trunk. They even sang "Oh Christmas Tree" as they admired its beauty. It was cut down quickly, in the cold and rain, on November 14, 1995.

> *The tree glittered with twenty-five thousand lights on another five miles of wiring, marking another breathtaking start to the Christmas season in New York City.*

When the majestic tree was lit on December 5, more than one hundred nuns were among the thousands of spectators in attendance to watch Christmas come to the Big

Apple. After their tree was taken down on January 3, 1996, it became an obstacle on a horse trail for the United States Equestrian Team, and the Sisters of Christian Charity have visited it there.

The 1995 Rockefeller Center Christmas tree was also immortalized in print. In 1996, Julie Salamon's novella *The Christmas Tree* was published. Based on Rockefeller Center's years-long courtship of the Mallinckrodt Convent's Norway spruce and its eventual trip to tower over New York City, the book fictionalizes some aspects of the story, but remains faithful to most of it, sometimes unintentionally. According to a *New York Times* article, Salamon's tree scout, Jesse King, was so like David Murbach that when Salamon met Murbach after her book's publication, she was certain she had met him somewhere before! It was only later that she realized she'd created a character just like him. Most importantly, though, *The Christmas Tree* captures the spirit of the actual story: kinship, giving, and holiday joy.

The 1995 Rockefeller Center Christmas tree was immortalized in print.

While the story of 1995's Christmas tree is especially heartwarming, the rest of the 1990s were rife with epic evergreen journeys whose stories are worth telling and retelling. In 1996, Ann Dilger, a retired secretary from Armonk, New York, donated a Norway spruce that had grown to a daunting ninety feet tall and forty-four feet wide! Dilger was first approached by Rockefeller Center tree officials to give up the tree in 1988, but she politely declined. The tree had been standing proudly on the property in 1951 when Dilger and her late husband moved into their home, and she was hesitant to part with it.

Eight years later, when center officials returned, she surrendered, deciding that the time had come to let go of the tree. Her children had counseled her and persuaded her that it would be a wonderful gesture to let others enjoy the tree in its last days. By that point, the tree was quite old, threatening to tumble onto her house the moment a bad storm passed through the region. Dilger made a shrewd deal: She received two thousand dollars for her tree, and landscapers replanted her yard, leaving her a dogwood, a rhododendron, and a fir (so that she would always have something green to admire during the winter).

Her evergreen took about a week to prepare and cut down, and during that time, police watched over Dilger's house in case protesters arrived to cause trouble. Hundreds of reporters, neighbors, and curious spectators watched as the tree was severed from its trunk in just a few minutes. Police then escorted the tree on its hundred-foot telescoping tractor-trailer into New York City. During the journey, the tree grazed a low-hanging sign at the toll plaza on the George Washington Bridge, but the precious evergreen remained undamaged. The enormous tree was decorated with a star and twenty-six thousand multicolored lights and enjoyed through the holiday season by millions of tourists and locals alike. It was finally taken down January 2 and donated to the Boy Scouts and the United States Equestrian Team to be recycled as logs and mulch.

Yet another Norway spruce made its way to Rockefeller Center in 1997, but this evergreen traveled in a way that none before it ever had: It arrived on a boat. Before its journey by sea, though, it seemed that fate had been the force that brought this tree to Manhattan. Many years before Rockefeller Center had inquired about a spruce on their property, Barbara and Vic Rickard already had discussed donating the very same tree to the plaza. Barbara had wanted to see her spruce become the national symbol of Christmas joy from the moment the Rickards bought their house in Stony Point, New York, but Vic had been against it. So the couple had dropped the matter, leaving the tree to flourish in their yard. The spruce had continued to grow . . . and grow . . . until it reached seventy-four feet in height.

The spruce was so tall that it caught Murbach's eye during an aerial tree-scouting trip in 1997. After landing his helicopter, he contacted the Rickards, who discussed the matter at length before reaching an agreement. Finally, they decided to donate the tree to Rockefeller Center for others to enjoy. They received a small honorarium, and landscapers planted a new tree in the old spruce's place. Then the real negotiations began: How would they transport the mammoth tree to Midtown Manhattan without damaging it? The tree that had struck the road sign the year before was still fresh in Murbach's mind, and he didn't want to take any chances.

Ultimately, it was decided that the Rickards' property was close enough to the Hudson River that it would be easiest to load the enormous tree onto a barge and send it down the river, bypassing tunnels, winding roads, and ever-present construction. Once the barge docked between the Manhattan and Brooklyn Bridges, the tree was loaded onto a tractor-trailer and driven into Midtown.

The tree arrived at the plaza on time and without

incident. It's a good thing, too, because 1997's lighting ceremony was an especially monumental event. It was televised live nationally for the first time and included performances by Kenny G, Harry Connick Jr., Dana Reeve, the Rockettes, Katarina Witt, and the entire cast of *Rent*. Bill Cosby pushed the button that illuminated the thousands of multicolored lights.

After the barge trip of 1997, it seemed that all avenues

had been explored in the way of innovative tree transport; however, the very next year ushered in another milestone when the evergreen arrived in Manhattan on the world's largest cargo plane! Hailing from a suburb of Cleveland, Ohio, it seemed curious that officials would need to look for a tree so far from New York.

Curious indeed. A four-day ice storm that began on January 7, 1997, pummeled the two spruces in upstate

In 1997, the Christmas tree arrived in Manhattan by sea.

New York that officials had been considering for 1998's Christmas tree. In fact, most of the evergreens in the area took quite a beating in the storms, and few were in any shape to become the most celebrated tree of the holiday season. So officials had to look elsewhere, and they ended up in Ohio, where they found a seventy-four-foot, seven-ton Norway spruce on the property of Ethel and Adolph Szitar that looked perfect for Christmas.

In fact, the tree had been the Szitars' actual indoor

The Rockettes performed at the tree lighting ceremony in 1997.

Christmas tree in the late 1930s, when it barely reached four feet in height. After the holidays, they had planted it in front of their ranch home in Richfield, Ohio, where it grew for sixty years. Center officials breathed a sigh of relief when they found the tree on April 15, 1998, just a few miles from John D. Rockefeller's birthplace; it was getting down to the wire, they needed a tree, and they'd already exhausted their usual tree-hunting grounds, even venturing as far north as Massachusetts.

Luckily, the Szitars were already contemplating the fate of their tree. They were beginning to experience that familiar anxiety common to most owners of aging evergreens: What if the tree falls on my house—or worse, me? So when Rockefeller Center officials offered the family free removal of the tree, the Szitars were thrilled. Officials even offered to plant a new Norway spruce in its place.

Then, of course, came the matter of transporting an enormous (yet somewhat delicate) spruce from Ohio to New York City in time for Christmas. This was a new conundrum for David Murbach, but he refused to be stumped. He knew that the evergreen would not be able to handle such a long distance in the bed of a tractor-trailer, and travel by barge proved just as impractical. Eventually Murbach settled on air travel. He located the world's largest cargo plane, the Antonov AN-124, which has a cargo hold 124 feet long. It was the first and only Rockefeller Center tree to come from the Midwest . . . and it was also the first and only Christmas tree to *fly* into New York City.

The tree made the trip from the Cleveland Hopkins International Airport to New York's Kennedy International Airport in mid-November after a send-off ceremony that included a speech by Cleveland Mayor Michael R. White and a performance by the Kent State Marching Band. Of course, the spruce was also met with much fanfare when it reached Manhattan; it was lit with twenty-six thousand

The world's largest cargo plane, the Antonov AN-124, flew a towering Norway spruce from Ohio to Manhattan in time for the Christmas celebration of 1998.

On December 2, 1998, the Christmas tree was lit with twenty-six thousand multicolored lights.

multicolored lights on December 2, 1998. Matt Lauer and Al Roker of the *Today* show hosted the nationally-televised, live ceremony, and Garth Brooks, Baby Face, Cyndi Lauper, Kristi Yamaguchi, and the Rockettes performed. Hillary Clinton was on hand to push the button that lit the tree, but perhaps the most important guests of all were Ethel Szitar and her family, who were flown to the Big Apple to attend the festivities.

After all the excitement of the previous few years, Rockefeller Center officials still managed to draw the decade—and the century—to a close with an unprecedented Rockefeller Center Christmas. In 1999, the plaza became the temporary home of the tallest tree ever to grace Manhattan: a one-hundred-foot Norway spruce from Killingworth, Connecticut. David Murbach had found this magnificent evergreen on an aerial survey in April. Fortunately, Murbach had little trouble convincing the owners, Jim and Cathy Thomson, that their ten-ton tree would be the perfect

The tree selected in 1999 stood at a remarkable one hundred feet tall.

Christmas centerpiece in Rockefeller Plaza; however, complications inevitably arose when the time came to transport the gigantic tree to Manhattan. Murbach realized that the spruce was too large to drive down Interstate 95 by truck, and it would never fit through the Lincoln Tunnel. Ultimately, he decided to attempt another journey by sea. The tree was felled and loaded onto a tractor-trailer as usual, but it was then taken to a ferry dock where fire engines hosed it down so that the full branches wouldn't be damaged by the salt water. Workers loaded it onto the ferry, where it floated to an aircraft carrier for a salute, and eventually made its way to Rockefeller Plaza. It was lit on December 1, 1999, a bitterly cold evening.

In 2003, another majestic Norway spruce became Rockefeller Plaza's Christmas centerpiece.

Chapter 9

TRADITION TODAY

As the spectacular trees and tree lighting ceremonies of the late 1990s illustrated, the Rockefeller Center Christmas tree was gaining more popularity and media attention with every passing year. By 2004, the tree was such an integral part of our collective holiday celebration that a mystery novel by Mary Higgins Clark centered around a plot to steal the tree from its home in Vermont!

Throughout the dawning of a new century, the spectacle continued to grow. Bigger stars, more famous headliners, taller trees, more elaborate lighting designs, and more advanced equipment made both selection and celebration of the tree all the more exciting in the new millennium.

In the 21ST century, David Murbach, tree-finder and gardens manager at Rockefeller Center, began using a global positioning system device to find potential Christmas trees! Of course, he still took several helicopter rides every year to get a bird's-eye view of the surrounding land, and he couldn't avoid the requisite driving trips to visit each tree in person (making sure they possessed that elusive "special something"). Using GPS technology, tree scouts maintain their incredibly high standards, but they spend less time searching for the perfect tree.

With extreme fame and fanfare, though, comes the inevitable envy and competition. For the Rockefeller Center Christmas tree, this means that other American cities have begun contending for the title of the grandest Christmas tree in the country.

Over the years, several United States cities have hoisted trees into their own town squares to be decorated and admired throughout the Christmas season, but none matched the grandeur of the Rockefeller Center Christmas tree . . . until 2002.

It all started in November, when a marketing company erected a Christmas tree on Biscayne Bay in Miami, Florida. The company and the mayor wanted to revitalize Miami's downtown, a decent place to work during the day but notoriously dull at night and on the weekends, with little tourist traffic. As new hotels, shops, and condominiums began to appear, though, it looked like Miami's downtown was starting to perk up. City officials had hoped that an enormous Norway spruce in the center of a Christmas village would spark holiday spirit (and the spending of tourist dollars).

So with the help of Egan Acres Tree Farm, Miami trucked in a 110-foot-tall, fifty-five-foot-wide Norway spruce from Yorktown Heights, New York, and proudly heralded it as the tallest Christmas tree in the country (Rockefeller

Biscayne Bay in Miami, Florida, erected a public Christmas tree of their own in 2002.

Center's tree was a mere seventy-six feet tall that year). The tree was about one hundred years old, so workers nailed dozens of supplemental branches to the aging spruce to give it a fuller appearance. Gardeners then went to great lengths to make sure the tree stayed green until Christmas. They coated it twice with pine tar base, which helps the needles retain water, and placed the tree in a large steel basin of water. The pampered evergreen also received daily sprays with a hose.

The tree was decorated with forty thousand multicolored lights on seven miles of wiring. A lighting ceremony was held, as well. A holiday village surrounded the tree, complete with an artificial skating rink, holiday scenes with cozy cottages, and manmade snow for making snowmen and snow angels. The only missing element was the cold weather!

Rockefeller Center officials insisted there was no competition when they heard about Miami's tree, but they did mention that Florida's tree did not possess the full sets of branches found on New York's celebrated trees. They also warned that the tree might dry out given the balmy weather in the Sunshine State, and they were right. By the week of Christmas, Miami's tree had turned brown, and a spot on the *Today* show featuring the Florida tree was canceled. Worse, tourists and locals alike lost interest in the withering Christmas tree.

In the meantime, the tree on Biscayne Bay was supplanted as the tallest. Newport Beach, California, erected a 112-foot white fir outside of its Fashion Island mall, announcing that it had the tallest and most attractive Christmas tree in the nation. Rockefeller Center refused to dispute the claims, though Miami and Newport Beach officials traded barbs in the press for several days. Despite their brief moments in the spotlight, these cities haven't made much of their Christmas displays in the years since 2002's rivalry; however, in Midtown Manhattan, Rockefeller Center's Christmas tree continues to dazzle onlookers every year without fail.

The 2000s

ROCKEFELLER CENTER KICKED OFF the new millennium with an eighty-foot Norway spruce that had been nurtured for fifty years in the front yard of Bill and Frances Heady's home in a small village in Westchester County. David Murbach had noticed the Headys' spruce three years before while searching for 1997's tree. Because he had already worked out deals for prospective Christmas trees until the end of the millennium, Murbach approached the Headys to ask if their spruce had any plans in three years' time. He assumed that with a strict regimen of water, fertilizer, and love, the Headys' tree would blossom into the perfect Christmas tree by 2000, and he was right.

By the time it was cut down in November of that year, the tree was eighty feet tall and forty-three feet wide, with branches dense enough that even the sun's rays couldn't shine through. The village of Buchanan was quite proud to have a native tree selected, and the Headys themselves, the heart of such a close community, were thrilled. Bill Heady had retired, but he formerly worked as the town's postmaster. His son also served the village, as a police officer. The family's home was guarded throughout early November to prevent any trouble, and the Headys received the customary sapling as well as a small honorarium for the gift of their tree.

The spruce starred in two ceremonies that year: First, on the day it was felled, New York Governor George Pataki made a speech and planted the new sapling in the old spruce's place as five hundred of the town's citizens looked on. The Headys' son also spoke as local media and politi-

The new millennium welcomed a dazzling Norway spruce into Rockefeller Center during the holidays.

cal officials bid farewell to the lovely tree. Then, after being adorned with thirty thousand twinkling lights, the tree was illuminated on November 29, 2000, amidst rain that did little to dampen the abundance of holiday joy present every year at the tree lighting ceremony.

To say that 2001 was a difficult year for New York City might be the understatement of the century. The terrorist attacks of September 11 shook the city and the nation to their core and sent millions of people into deep mourning. Still, no one doubted that New York would retain its joyful spirit, and that the Christmas tradition in Rockefeller Center would live on in 2001. An eighty-one-foot Norway spruce that had been selected by David Murbach in April was triumphantly erected in Rockefeller Plaza during the holiday season.

Andrew and Kelly Tornabene of Wayne, New Jersey, donated their eighty-year-old, eight-ton tree, a lovely specimen that had drawn

The holiday festivities of 2001 helped restore a sense of hope and joy to the people of New York City.

them to their property twelve years before. The Tornabenes were glad to give up their tree, even though they had to temporarily relocate their garage to remove it from their yard. They were honored that their tree would serve as the Christmas centerpiece during a time when the nation needed a symbol of hope and cheer.

The Tornabenes traveled to Manhattan for the tree lighting ceremony on November 28, 2001, which honored the victims of the terrorist attacks as well as the thousands of rescue workers who toiled tirelessly throughout the fall of that year. Security measures were heightened, of course, and more police officers than in previous years were on hand to make sure the evening stayed calm and bright. The décor was altered slightly, too. Rather than the customary silver banners, American flags were hung throughout the plaza, and the lights on the tree—which were usually multicolored—sparkled red, white, and blue. No one seemed to mind; in fact, the hundreds of thousands of spectators were somber but festive as they observed the ceremony, the balmy sixty-degree temperatures helping to lighten the mood.

First Lady Laura Bush spoke at the ceremony in 2001, as did New York Mayor Rudolph Giuliani. Destiny's Child, Marc Anthony, and John Mellencamp performed live, while Jewel, Tony Bennett, and the Rockettes performed in previously taped showcases that were displayed in the square on large television screens. Bush and Giuliani flipped the candy-cane switch that illuminated the tree amidst a swell of patriotic pride and holiday joy.

In 2002, the first and only year that marked competitions among the nation's public Christmas celebrations, Rockefeller Center's tree was just as stunning as always. David Murbach selected a seventy-six-foot Norway spruce from Bloomsbury, New Jersey, to stand in the plaza. With its flawless triangular shape and full branch spread, the evergreen put the other cities' trees to shame. Before arriving in the Big Apple, the spruce had been blocking the driveway of Carmine and Mary Rizzo, and they were glad to have it removed and put to such festive use. At seventy years old and forty-four feet wide at its base, the center's 2002 tree stayed lush and green throughout the holidays, holding itself regally above the skaters on the pond and the shoppers in the streets. After it was taken down in January, the wood from the tree was used to make toy animals.

Manchester, Connecticut, reared the Norway spruce that became the Rockefeller Center Christmas tree in 2003. In April, center officials knocked on the door of Frances

Despite the competition from other cities across the nation, 2002's Christmas tree was no less spectacular.

Katkauskas, who lived with her son, Andy, on the five and a half acres her family has owned for eighty years. She and her late husband had planted the tree in 1953, and in fifty years, it had grown to seventy-nine feet, with a forty-three-foot branch spread at its widest point. The evergreen weighed in at a hefty nine tons. It made a fine sight for holiday revelers to admire throughout the Christmas season, and it was lit every evening until January 6, 2004, when it was recycled into chips to cover the Appalachian Trail.

The Swarovski star is nine feet wide and weighs 550 pounds.

In 2004, the unveiling of the Swarovski crystal star (which would top the tree annually from that moment forward) was perhaps more exciting than that of the tree itself. Created in Austria by a team of designers, the star is the largest that has ever sat atop the Rockefeller Center Christmas tree. At nine feet in diameter and 550 pounds, this masterpiece twinkles with twenty-five thousand tiny crystals.

The tree itself was rather spectacular that year, too. Reaching seventy-one feet in height and forty feet in width, it weighed in at nine tons. The spruce made the journey from the home of Christine Gabrielibes and Demos Kontos in Suffern, New York, on a tractor-trailer and then a barge. Glowing with thirty thousand bulbs, the tree was celebrated in another impressive ceremony on November 30, 2004. Olympians Sarah Hughes, an ice skater, and Paul Hamm and Carly Patterson, gymnasts, lit the tree along with the mayor. Clay Aiken and Jessica Simpson sang Christmas carols, and tourists from around the globe gathered to enjoy the start of the holiday season.

In 2005, soon after hurricanes Rita and Katrina ravaged the nation's coasts, Americans looked again to the joyous festivities of Christmas in New York City to lift their spirits during a devastating time. That year, children displaced by the hurricanes joined Harry Connick Jr., a New Orleans native, and New York Mayor Michael Bloomberg at the tree lighting ceremony. But 2005's guest of honor was a seventy-four-foot Norway spruce from Wayne, New Jersey, and another set of thirty thousand lights only made the tree more splendid. Its forty-two-foot branch span glittered magically as Earth, Wind & Fire, Sheryl Crow, Rod Stewart, and The Brian Setzer Orchestra performed. The ceremony was nationally televised on NBC, and *Today* show personality Al Roker, along with Megan Mullally of *Will & Grace*, hosted the event.

Roker hosted the ceremony again in 2006 when a Norway spruce from Ridgefield, Connecticut, served as the plaza's Christmas centerpiece. It was the tallest tree to have graced Rockefeller Plaza in years. It stood a full eighty-eight feet tall and forty-five feet wide at its broadest point. Weighing nine tons, the tree was estimated to be between seventy and eighty years old.

The tree for 2006 was illuminated November 29 with thirty thousand multicolored lights on five miles of wire and topped with the Swarovski star for the third year in a row. Ann Curry of the *Today* show joined Roker as hosts for the ceremony, which was broadcast on NBC. The celebration

The Swarovski star made its debut atop the Rockefeller Center Christmas tree in 2004.

featured performances by Sting, Enya, Christina Aguilera, Lionel Richie, Sarah McLachlan, Martina McBride, and John Legend, who sang Christmas favorites to the delighted crowd.

Illuminated toy soldiers make a festive addition to the plaza's decorations.

The following year marked another milestone for the Rockefeller Center Christmas tree: It was the year the tree truly went green. The center switched from thirty thousand regular lights to solar-powered L.E.D. lights on five miles of wire, which saved about thirteen hundred kilowatt-hours per day in energy (enough to power a medium-sized house for an entire month!). The light-emitting diodes are powered by solar panels that top 45 Rockefeller Plaza. Because these special lights do not have filaments that burn out, they last an exceptionally long time. They also produce no heat, which makes them safer than traditional electrical lights.

Adding to the green theme, the tree was felled using a handheld saw for the first time in fifty years. Also, after 2007's tree was taken down, it was cut into boards, treated, and donated to Habitat for Humanity for use in building projects for needy families all over the world.

But what about the tree itself? The eighty-four-foot, nine-ton Norway spruce hailed from Shelton, Connecticut. Joseph and Judy Rivnyak donated the tree after being approached in the summer of 2007 by Rockefeller Center officials. After agreeing to donate the evergreen, they became local celebrities in their New England hamlet. The spruce was nurtured through the autumn and transported to New York City on a one-hundred-foot trailer.

It was lit on November 28, 2007, in a ceremony hosted by Nick Lachey, Al Roker, and Ashley Tisdale, who flipped the switch to illuminate the tree. Celine Dion, Carrie Underwood, and Tony Bennett belted out Christmas carols, and the event was once again broadcast nationally on NBC. The Rivnyaks attended, having been escorted by center officials into Manhattan in a limousine. While they enjoyed being treated like royalty, they truly just felt honored to have been such an integral part of the Rockefeller Center Christmas tree tradition.

In 2008, a seventy-two-foot tall Norway spruce from Hamilton, New Jersey graced Rockefeller Center. When Mary Kremper and her husband planted the tree (which happened to be their first Christmas tree together) nearly eighty years ago, back in 1931, she predicted that it would one day become Rockefeller Center's Christmas centerpiece . . . and she was right. While she and her husband did not live to see their tree arrive in New York City, their twin sons, Bill and Bob Varanyak, were thrilled to see their mother's dreams fulfilled. The tree was lit on December 3, 2008, during a star-studded celebration that featured performances by Beyonce, David Cook, Faith Hill, Tony Bennett, Harry Connick Jr., and even the Jonas Brothers.

In 2009, the Rockefeller Center Christmas tree shined brighter than ever when the five-year-old Swarovski star that crowns the tree got a tune-up. The new star was unveiled at the December 2nd lighting ceremony with musical accompaniment from artists like Aretha Franklin and Shakira. It dazzled visitors with an additional 720 LEDs: miniature one-watt white light bulbs powered by an impressive 3,000

An 80-year-old Norway spruce served as the Rockefeller Center Christmas tree in 2008.

feet of wire hidden within the star itself. A seventy-six-foot-tall Norway spruce from Easton, CT was the tree chosen to show off the newly refurbished star. The impressive evergreen was donated by a local fifth-grade teacher, Maria Corti, who credits her tree's stature to the fertile location where it grew: over a septic tank!

Sadly, 2009's festivities were marked by the tragic loss of David Murbach, the man who had been the behind-the-scenes star of the Rockefeller Center Christmas tradition for over a quarter of a century. Only 57 years old, Murbach passed away at his home in Florida on December 23. Settling for nothing less than perfection, Murbach had dedicated himself to the annual year-round search for the iconic tree for decades and focused on little else until that tree was found in time for each holiday celebration. Serving as the manager of the gardens division at Rockefeller Center, Murbach also filled the position of tending some of the world's most celebrated urban gardens. He will be missed immensely, but his life's work will live on in the tradition of the Rockefeller Center Christmas tree.

The last tree chosen by David Murbach glitters in Rockefeller Center in December 2009.

A Norway spruce from Ridgefield, Connecticut, served as the plaza's Christmas centerpiece in 2006.

Chapter 10

THE FUTURE OF TRADITION

According to the National Christmas Tree Association, the first documented Christmas tree was decorated in Riga, Latvia, in 1510—nearly five hundred years ago! The modern Christmas tree with which we are familiar didn't make its way to the United States until the nineteenth century, when German emigrants introduced a tabletop variety. The popularity of these petit Christmas trees spread, and soon large numbers of families began bringing taller models into their homes during the holiday season. These Christmas trees became so popular that the natural supply dwindled dangerously. As a result, the first Christmas tree farm was established in New Jersey in 1901. And the rest, as they say, is history.

The tradition of the Christmas tree, whether real or artificial and whether public or private, endures, and there

Every year, millions of families decorate evergreens in their homes to celebrate Christmas.

are certainly no plans to discontinue the true harbinger of Christmas in New York City: the lighting of the Rockefeller Center Christmas tree. This celebrated symbol of the holidays remains a beloved tradition seventy-five years after its inception.

In the years since the Rockefeller Center construction workers of the Great Depression decorated a small tree at their building site (in celebration not only of the holiday but also of their employment), the hope and goodwill that the tree initially embodied has persevered. Although the Rockefeller Center Christmas tree lighting ceremony is televised now, and center officials use advanced technology to find the perfect tree, the spirit of joy that was present at the plaza's first simple Christmas celebration still remains.

> *This celebrated symbol of the holidays remains a beloved tradition seventy-five years after its inception.*

APPENDIX:
A TREE TIMELINE

▲ A TREE TIMELINE ▲

Year	Size	Species	Origin
1931	20-foot	balsam	
1933	50-foot	balsam	
1934	70-foot	Norway spruce	Babylon, New York
1935	80-foot	Norway spruce	Babylon, New York
1936	70 feet each	Two Norway spruces	private estate, Morristown, New Jersey
1937	70 feet each	Two Norway spruces	Peter Stuyvesant estate, Allamuchy, New York
1938	70-foot	Norway spruce	
1939	75-foot	Norway spruce	estate in New Jersey
1940	88-foot	Norway spruce	William Eastwood estate, Dutchess County, New York
1941	83-foot	Norway spruce	
1942	50-foot center, 30 feet on each side	Three living Norway spruce	Huntington, New York
1943	55-foot living	Norway spruce	
1944	65-foot living	Norway spruce	estate on West Islip, New York
1945	55-foot living	Norway spruce	Syosset, New York
1946	75-foot	Norway spruce	Syosset Nurseries, Long Island, New York
1947	65-foot	Norway spruce	farm in Dear Park, New York

♠ A TREE TIMELINE ♠			
Year	Size	Species	Origin
1948	90-foot	Norway spruce	Mr. and Mrs. Carll Tucker, Mt. Kisco, New York
1949	75-foot	Norway spruce	Yaphank, New York
1950	85-foot	Norway spruce	Hollingsworth Wood estate, Mt. Kisco, New York
1951	82-foot	Norway spruce	Lake Ronkonkoma, New York
1952	85-foot	Norway spruce	Peter Stuyvesant estate, Allamuchy, New York
1953	75-foot	Norway spruce	William P. Jenks, Morristown, New Jersey
1954	65-foot	Norway spruce	Belvidere, New Jersey
1955	65-foot	Norway spruce	Belvidere, New Jersey
1956	64-foot	white spruce	Charles W. Elliott, Whitefield, New Hampshire
1957	65-foot	white spruce	Mr. and Mrs. Maurice Plante, Island Pond, Vermont
1958	64-foot	white spruce	East Madison, Maine
1959	70-foot	Norway spruce	Alva Silliman, Podunk, Massachusetts
1960	65-foot	Norway spruce	Mr. and Mrs. Emanuel Owens, Harford, Pennsylvania

	♠ A TREE TIMELINE ♠		
Year	Size	Species	Origin
1961	85-foot	Norway spruce	Mr. And Mrs. M.A. Gilmartin Jr., Smithtown, New York
1962	67-foot	white spruce	Scott Paper Co. Greenville Junction, Maine
1963	60-foot	Norway spruce	Dr. and Mrs. Elbert J. Loughran, Hurley, New York
1964	60-foot	Norway spruce	Mr. and Mrs. Vito D'Auria, Lake Carmel, New York
1965	60-foot	Norway spruce	Mr. and Mrs. Charles Fagg, Darien, Connecticut
1966	64-foot	white spruce	Canadian government, Petawawa Forest, Canada
1967	65-foot	balsam	Coventry, Vermont
1968	55-foot	white spruce	Holland, Vermont
1969	70-foot	balsam	Saranac Lake, New York
1970	60-foot	white spruce	Coventry, Vermont
1971	65-foot	balsam	Robert Bragg farm, East Montpelier, Vermont
1972	65-foot	Norway spruce	Old Bridge, New Jersey
1973	65-foot	Norway spruce	Tenafly, New Jersey
1974	63-foot	Norway spruce	Lehighton, Pennsylvania

▲ A TREE TIMELINE ▲

Year	Size	Species	Origin
1975	59-foot	balsam	Jean Wolfe, New Canaan, Connecticut
1976	65-foot	Norway spruce	Florence and Edward Praisner, Montclair, New Jersey
1977	65-foot	white spruce	Dixfield, Maine
1978	75-foot	Norway spruce	Immaculate Conception Seminary, Mahwah, New Jersey
1979	65-foot	Norway spruce	Spring Valley, New York
1980	65-foot	Norway spruce	Charles Mapes, Suffern, New York
1981	65-foot	white spruce	West Danville, Vermont
1982	70-foot	Norway spruce	Immaculate Conception Seminary, Mahwah, New Jersey
1983	75-foot	Norway spruce	Mr. and Mrs. Allan Heinsohn, Valley Cottage, New York
1984	75-foot	Norway spruce	Far Hills, New Jersey
1985	75-foot	Norway spruce	Richard and Diane Dohl, Harveyville, Pennsylvania
1986	68-foot	Norway spruce	Mary and Vinnie Froeling, Nanuet, New York
1987	75-foot	Norway spruce	Charles Mapes, Suffern, New York

♠ A TREE TIMELINE ♠

Year	Size	Species	Origin
1988	75-foot	Norway spruce	Rich and Lynn Luster, Raritan Township, New Jersey
1989	70-foot	Norway spruce	John Myers, Suffern, New York
1990	75-foot	Norway spruce	Shirley Cenci, West Norwalk, Connecticut
1991	65-foot	Norway spruce	Charles Mapes, Suffern, New York
1992	65-foot	Norway spruce	Andrew Kupusinkis, Stony Point, New York
1993	85-foot	Norway spruce	Raymond and Marie Cronin, Nanuet, New York
1994	85-foot	Norway spruce	Maria and Alan Eglar, Ridgefield, Connecticut
1995	75-foot	Norway spruce	Mallinckrodt Convent, Mendham, New Jersey
1996	90-foot	Norway spruce	Ann Dilger, Armonk, New York
1997	74-foot	Norway spruce	Barbara and Vic Rickard, Stony Point, New York
1998	74-foot	Norway spruce	Ethel and Adolph Szitar, Richfield, Ohio
1999	100-foot	Norway spruce	Jim and Cathy Thomson, Killingworth, Connecticut

A TREE TIMELINE

Year	Size	Species	Origin
2000	80-foot	Norway spruce	Bill and Frances Heady, Buchanan, New York
2001	81-foot	Norway spruce	Andrew and Kelly Tornabene, Wayne, New Jersey
2002	76-foot	Norway spruce	Carmine and Mary Rizzo, Bloomsbury, New Jersey
2003	79-foot	Norway spruce	Frances Katkauskas, Manchester, Connecticut
2004	71-foot	Norway spruce	Christine Gabrielibes and Demos Kontos, Suffern, New York
2005	74-foot	Norway spruce	Wayne, New Jersey
2006	88-foot	Norway spruce	Ridgefield, Connecticut
2007	84-foot	Norway spruce	Joseph and Judy Rivnyak, Shelton, Connecticut
2008	72-foot	Norway spruce	Mary Kremper and Joseph Varanyak, Hamilton, New Jersey
2009	76-foot	Norway spruce	Maria Corti, Easton, Connecticut

LIST OF WORKS CONSULTED

Ames, Lynne. 1996. A Towering Tree Joins Skyscrapers for Christmas, and Fame. *The New York Times*, Dec. 22.

Anderson, Susan Heller, and David W. Dunlap. 1985. New York Day by Day: Bogged Down. *The New York Times*, Nov. 23.

Anonymous. Winter 2002. Lighting Up. *American Forests*, 107 (4): 20.

Anonymous. Winter 2004. 'Tis the Season. *American Forests*, 109 (4): 15.

Augostini, Louis. 1960. Pa. Landmark to Fall for New York. *Evening Press*.

Barron, James. 1997. Tree Taking River Trip To Rockefeller Center. *The New York Times*, Nov. 10.

Barron, James. 1999. Public Lives. *The New York Times*, Aug. 20.

Boland Jr., Ed. 2002. F.Y.I.: Big Thirsty Tree? *The New York Times*, Dec. 22.

Bruni, Frank. 1995. After Years of Saying No, Nuns Give Up Evergreen; A New Jersey Convent's Prized Spruce Is Becoming Rockefeller Center's Tree. *The New York Times*, Nov. 13.

Canedy, Dana. 2002. For the Snowbird, a Tree To Top Rockefeller's. *The New York Times*, Nov. 25.

Catskill Mountain Star. 1963. Rockefeller Center Tree To Come From Hurley. Aug. 29.

Centerscope: Rockefeller Center Inc. 1965. It's a Beauty . . . From the Nutmeg State. Nov. 18.

Collins, Glenn. 1998. Christmas, This Year, From Cleveland; Ice Storm Leads to Wide Search For a Spruce for Rockefeller Center. *The New York Times*, Nov. 5.

Cummings, Betsy. 2004. A Tree Worthy of Rockefeller Center. *The New York Times*, Nov. 28.

D'Agostino, Carla Torsilieri, and Byron Keith Byrd. *The Christmas Tree at Rockefeller Center.* New York: Lickle Publishing, 1997.

DeMasters, Karen. 2000. Now It's Six Horses Leaping. *The New York Times*, Jan. 16.

Deutsch, Claudia H. 1999. A Group Without a Center; Rockefeller Investment Arm Trying Not To Look Back. *The New York Times*, Dec. 1.

Foderaro, Lisa W. 2000. A Village's Tree to Shine as City Star. *The New York Times*, Nov. 9.

Fording, Laura. 2000. Oh Christmas Tree – Once it lived a quiet, unassuming life in Westchester County. Now it's the main attraction. How the Rockefeller Center Christmas Tree came to be. *Newsweek*, Dec. 8.

Gates, Anita. 2005. What's On Tonight. *The New York Times*, Nov. 30.

Hoffman, Jan. 1999. Public Lives; Behind Every Great Tree, or Some, Is a Man. *The New York Times*, Nov. 16.

Holtz, Jeff. 2003. Worth Noting; Bright Lights, Big City: The Journey of a Tree. *The New York Times*, Nov. 16.

Knight, Michael. 1975. A Neighborhood's Tree Goes Off to the Big City. *The New York Times*, Nov. 20.

Krebs, Albin. 1982. Notes on People; A Perennial Tree Is Returned to the Earth. *The New York Times*, Jan. 5.

Kuntzman, Gersh. 2002. American Beat: Oy, Tannenbaum. *Newsweek*, Dec. 23.

Lang, David. 1981. W. Danville Tree Going To Rockefeller Plaza.

Leuck, Thomas J. 2001. The Red, White and Blue Dominates Tree Lighting. *The New York Times*, Nov. 29.

Martin, Douglas. 1994. A Gardener Whose Tree Ushers In Christmas. *The New York Times*, Dec. 2.

Martin, Douglas. 2007. Marc Torsilieri, 48, Provider of Annual Christmas Tree, Is Dead. *The New York Times*, March 17.

McGill, Douglas C. 1983. It's Beginning to Look A Lot Like Christmas. *The New York Times*. Dec. 2.

Mifflin, Lawrie. 1997. TV Notes; Tree City, U.S.A. *The New York Times*, Dec. 3.

New York Times. 1934. Rockefeller Center Gets A 70-Foot Tree. Dec. 10.

New York Times. 1939. 75-Foot Yule Tree Set Up. Dec. 15.

New York Times. 1941. 4 Reindeer To Visit the City for Christmas; They Will Browse in Rockefeller Center. Dec. 1.

New York Times. 1945. Snow Adds Traditional Touch of Yuletide As Lights Go on at Rockefeller Plaza Tree. Dec. 15.

New York Times. 1948. 90-Foot Yule Tree Put Up In 7 Hours. Dec. 2.

New York Times. 1948. Mount Kisco Yule Tree Will Bring Pleasure to Millions. Dec. 2, Mt. Kisco edition.

New York Times. 1951. Yule Really Here; Plaza Tree Is Up. Dec. 4.

New York Times. 1954. Rockefeller Center's 22d Annual Christmas Tree, a 65-Foot Spruce, Goes Into Place in Teeth of High Winds. Nov. 30.

New York Times. 1955. About New York: 65-Foot Spruce for Center Mall Enters City Today. Nov. 28.

New York Times. 1956. Christmas Tree Rises In Midtown. Nov. 27.

New York Times. 1959. Topics: Gift from Massachusetts. Dec. 19.

New York Times. 1961. Christmas Glow Spread Over City. Dec. 8.

New York Times. 1964. Holiday Forerunner Arrives Here. Dec. 1.

New York Times. 1979. Protester Climbs Rockefeller Tree. Dec. 27.

New York Times. 1980. Tree-Climber Arrested at Rockefeller Center. Dec. 10.

New York Times. 1987. New Yorker Seeks Symbol of Season. Nov. 15.

New York Times. 1991. A True Tree, A Tree's Tree, A Tree to See. Nov. 29.

New York Times. 1992. Christmas Tree's Fate: Helping Life as Mulch. Jan. 9.

Nevard, Jacques. 1966. Christmases Past—and Present. *The New York Times,* Nov. 30.

Okrent, Daniel. *Great Fortune: The Epic of Rockefeller Center.* New York: Penguin, 2003.

Philadelphia Inquirer. 1960. Columnist Up a Tree, Governor Out on Limb. Nov. 20.

Phillips, McClandish. 1963. Rockefeller Center Starts Christmas Shopping. *The New York Times.* Aug. 23.

Ramunni, Kate. 2007. Shelton Tree Spruces Up Rockefeller Center. *Connecticut Post, Bridgeport,* Nov. 29.

Raver, Anne. 1993. The Search, Even by Air, for a '94 Tree. *The New York Times,* Dec. 23.

Robbins, Dale Bennett. 1972. Letter to the Editor: Save Radio City's Xmas Tree. *The New York Times,* Oct. 17.

Rockefeller Center Monthly. 1940. Front Page. December.

Rockefeller Center Monthly. 1942. Front Page. December.

Rockefeller Center Weekly. 1935. What We'll Do For Christmas. Dec. 17.

Rockefeller Center Weekly. 1936. It's On the Ice! Dec. 19.

Salamon, Julie. *The Christmas Tree: A Story of the Rockefeller Center Tree.* New York: Random House, 1996.

LIST OF WORKS CONSULTED

Salamon, Julie. 2003. Christmas Carols; First she created him, and then she met him: A true tale of the Rockefeller Center tree. *The New York Times*, Dec. 21.

Sawyer, Mina Titus. 1958. Maine's Magnificent Spruce. *Lewiston-Auburn, Maine Journal*, Dec. 20.

Schneider, Daniel B. 1996. F.Y.I.; Let There Be Black Light. *The New York Times*, Nov. 24.

Shattuck, Kathryn. 2001. For Young Viewers; Tall Enough For the World To See. *The New York Times*, Nov. 25.

Shattuck, Kathryn. 2006. What's On Wednesday Night. *The New York Times*, Nov. 29.

Shattuck, Kathryn. 2007. What's On Tonight. *The New York Times*, Nov. 28.

Smith, J. Stephen. 2007. Dreaming of a Green Christmas. *Newsday*, Dec. 9.

Strauss, Robert. 2003. A Christmas Tale. *The New York Times*, Dec. 7.

Tishman Speyer. *The Tree at Rockefeller Center: A Holiday Tradition*. New York: Tishman Speyer, 2007.

Voice of America News. 2007. Christmas Goes Green. Dec. 18.

About Cider Mill Press

Good ideas ripen with time. From seed to harvest, Cider Mill Press strives to bring fine reading, information, and entertainment together between the covers of its creatively crafted books. Our Cider Mill bears fruit twice a year, publishing a new crop of titles each Spring and Fall.

Visit us on the web at
www.cidermillpress.com
or write to us at
12 Port Farm Road
Kennebunkport, Maine 04046